RIGHTEOUS IRE
OF THE REINCARNATED
JETHRO TULL

Tim Richardson

LIVE CANON

For Eleanor

Love, Tim Richardson

First Published in 2015
By Live Canon Ltd
www.livecanon.co.uk

All rights reserved

© Tim Richardson 2015

978-1-909703-10-0

The right of Tim Richardson to be identified as author of this work has been asserted by him in accordance with Section 77 of the Copyright, Design and Patents Act 1988.

All rights reserved. No part of this publication may be reproduced, stored in or introduced into a retrieval system, or transmitted, in any form, or by any means (electronic, mechanical, photocopying, recording or otherwise) without the prior written permission of the publisher. Any person who does any unauthorized act in relation to this publication may be liable to criminal prosecution and civil claims for damages.

A CIP catalogue record for this book is available from the British Library.

This book is sold subject to the condition that it shall not, by way of trade or otherwise, be lent, re-sold, hired out, or otherwise circulated without the publisher's prior consent in any form of binding or cover other than that in which it is published and without a similar condition including this condition being imposed on the subsequent purchaser.

Edited by Helen Eastman for Live Canon
www.livecanon.co.uk

RIGHTEOUS IRE
OF THE REINCARNATED
JETHRO TULL

Tim Richardson is a London-based journalist and author specialising in the history of landscape and contemporary urban design; his fourteen books in this area include *The Arcadian Friends: Inventing the English Landscape Garden* (2007). He writes a regular column on gardens in *The Daily Telegraph*. Tim also advises the National Trust on landscape conservation and is the author of Oxford University's course on the history of the English landscape garden. He is the founder-director of the Chelsea Fringe, the volunteer-run alternative gardens festival.

Tim began writing poetry in 2010, at which point he attended a six-month course at the Faber Academy under the tutelage of Jo Shapcott and Daljit Nagra. He spent the next four years meeting bi-weekly with the Lamb Poets in Bloomsbury, London, treating each meeting as a deadline for a new poem. This is his first collection of poetry.

Contents

Storm over Settignano	7
The Invention of Chicken Marengo	8
red bird	10
moon	11
Notes on the Doric	12
b1c3	14
9pm	15
Righteous Ire of the Reincarnated Jethro Tull	16
'A Vase of Flowers'	17
from the castle	18
Grindelwald	19
Topographical Guide to the Nymphs of Great Britain and Ireland	20
The Australian	27
Welcombe Mouth	29
18/19	32
Broadmoor Sirens	33
Pick-a-dee	35
Lucy Rie Bakes a Cake	37
old place	38
the boys	39
Landscape With Too Few Lovers (1986)	42
May Day in Dayton	43

the return of the yellow-robed monk	44
That French Novel	47
Gallery Girl	48
Experimental Lady Poets of the 1920s	49
To William Shenstone	50
How to Spend It	51
Examination of the Wengler Sisters in the Lecture Theatre of the Museum of Natural History, University of Leiden, March 15th 1762	52
Peter?	54
Valete	55
At Asheham	56
Back Story	57
QUIET FOR THE WOUNDED	58
Maison Awkward	59
Endsleigh Pink	60
Camden Morning	61
A Bowl of Fruit	62

Storm over Settignano

Santissima Annunziata
is springing leaks
naked on its hillside
a lunatic nun, losing it

millisecond nymphs
sent by the goddess Paparazzi
flit through the olives
tantalising swains

in a dainty side-chapel
pink frescoes are streaking
while outside the fields
stand lithograph black

this landscape is pathetic
say the nymphs
as they bathe in the waters
evaporating at dawn

The Invention of Chicken Marengo

Boom! There go the Austrians.
The reporters say it sounds like thunder but
artillery is not a meteorological phenomenon —
it's a concatenation of splintered wood,
stone and any old shit it hits and then
redistributes at high speed in all directions,
dispersing atoms in a way approved of
by Clairaut and Lagrange. You seem surprised.
I read the greats when I studied medicine
which is also, by the way, where I learned
the principles and methods of dissection
that I now apply to fish and fowl and —
when we can get it — sides of fresh flesh
whose nodules and tendons require the ministrations
of knife number one which I guarantee
will outstrip the sabre of any one of those
shitty cuirassiers from the Midi (peasants in fancy dress).
My master favours poultry and he eats it standing up.
I will cook for him any time of day or night and he knows it.
And if Kellermann or another wants a cherry sauce
then the Vice-Consul of the Republique de France
will tell him to fuck off on my behalf just like he did
the other night. So why don't you fuck off
and go and find me a proper cock-bird
which I can truss and roast so it's ready
just as soon as he leaps from his horse,
so he can hold its white breast in a napkin,
the plan of battle laid out before him,
a piquant sauce of capers in this dish here
for slathering 'til it drips down the wrists.
There is nothing a hairy Hungarian grenadier likes better
than shoving his bayonet right up a little dragoon's arse.
So you had better get moving, is what I am saying.

I do not think I exaggerate when I observe that
my mutton ragout won him the Battle of the Pyramids.
He sucked at the the bones, which is how they eat
on the islands and is a noble gustation, and spat out
that white end, all the while savouring my salting
and pursing his lips, and pointed straight-armed
with the meat in his hand, saying, 'Turn the division like so!'
That's what did it. A general who eats before battle
could never think of such a thing, and any officer
who goes out full-bellied will get his guts spilled,
mark my words. But it's not my place to tell them —
they have to find out for themselves, like Duclos
who scoffed our only good bread at Jaffa
then got half his side blown off and had to lie there
bleeding into the dirt waiting for the Turk to come
and cut off his balls. What a kitchen! A complete shithole.
But sniff this tomato. And look at the size of these crayfish!
Ah, 'Pack-a-ti-pack-a!' There goes the infantry, clearing their tubes.
We're on! That volley sounded like a game of skittles —
they'll get a bollocking. And yes I know I always say it but:
'Victory is in the Air!' Get those pans boiling!
This morning we are making something special.

red bird

he said the skin would slip off

didn't mention the smell

the head hanging there

the way the feathers fell

the crack of the ankle

the insinuation

in the special place

as he peeled the skin

crimson guts

until he held the red bird

a shining bird

like pyjamas

of dead blood

and the beak

like a coronet

which had to be done

of a finger

under the belly

from the breast

lolloping

in one hand

without pyjamas

moon

on the beach
  soft grey fossils
      are trampled by rain

in the house
  the author regards
      oeufs en cocotte

out at sea
  a million mussels
      opening

Notes on the Doric

For making a plain Cieling, Cornice and plain Stucco to Walls	£11 : 15s : 0d
For 4 round frames, mending and putting up the Basso-Relievos to Ditto Temple	£1 : 12s : 0d
For the additional ornaments over the Basso-Relievos	£4 : 4s : 0d

squat and *four-square* with *recessed portico*
(photograph by the author)
the *ball finials* something more than a consolation
a *Serlian flourish* on a *uniformly dull pediment*
with *copybook columns* straight from Ware
and nary even a *taper* or *flute*
so what shall we do with these bloody macaronis?

a brace of gilded Neapolitans shipped over
to glister Blenheim's saloon, staircase and hall
fed bread and broth on the scaff and then
this little Doric number down the road
this little slum-it-and-go tucked into an English lawn
where confused foreign gods shiver in dirty togas
wishing they could quit this damp embassy to barbarism
these sodden fields and crow-strewn copses
find instead a pavilion whose line and proportion
might honour their old stories and perfectible dusks

> a temple of ancient worthies
> a pantheon in the haze
> a dripping nymphaeum
> a kinky rotunda

even a grotto would suffice – anywhere but this
dullard's dream of Arcady, this pretentious shack

so Mazzini father and son straight off the packet
then down the turnpike to finish it in situ
and on in the mud to this cut-price country coz
getting shouted at all day long –
remember the monks Antonio, *'Ora et Labora!'* –
by some wannabe milordi who didn't even have the
gumption to get to Rome not even in the '50s
but sits counting his woodcock while dreaming
of iced-cream in trompe-l'oeiled trellises dandling
dimpled bosomy giggly girls with cochineally lips

at Ditchley
a cool wind insinuates
a room that is filled
with noise
and its remains

it is not a notable example of the genre

b1c3

glowing like horses
coming to rest
tensile misgivings strewn
along cross-hatched pebbleways

                only so much paper ephemera
                acres of Prince of Wales check

when I asked you what the problem was
you backed away
hid
then retreated via a gradient

                celadon mementoes

later on
when I knew it was pen-
ultimate

                and picked out your sand eyes

                                  a l l

                the scrape of wood and wood

                                t h o s e

                your knight errant

                                  p e o p l e

9pm

halogen snow appears
warming the gardens
lighting hunched shrubs
as by a flicked switch
teetering round fenceposts
like a tightrope walker
while everywhere
the engine of its tragic press
  squeaks
        creaks
and on the staircase
there was a dead fox
I saw it plain
and it was the light
from the snow

Righteous Ire of the Reincarnated Jethro Tull

I own three hundred and eighty six books.
I am not a bumpkin. I was famous
across Warwickshire for my repartee,
entertaining gentlemen (and ladies)
in my green leather-upholstered salon.
My household was renowned for its dessert:
sugared fruit glistening on mahogany.
I rode out on a dappled grey gelding,
my poor lungs supping up the sweet spring air.
And the hunt would meet at my house. My house.

In the fields I was Varro, Alcinous,
Columella at once. You know nothing
of what I speak. A virtuous farmer,
I saw good seed wasted in dead furrows
where fools cast away their masters' money.
My machine, my contraption, my invention —
the labouring men wanted to destroy it,
always moaning: 'But the old ways are best'.
Scribblers said I had not read my Virgil.
My riposte: 'What, then, of crop rotation?'

I told them this fairy tale (a fabrication!)
'Wheezing in my pew, I saw seeds not sounds
in the organ's pipes. Thus came my seed drill.'
How smoothly it read in the pages of
the *Gentleman's Magazine* that August.
Coke took one, then the Chancellor himself.
And they said I'd never read the Georgics!
My beets were the fattest from Warwickshire
to Norfolk. My corn: as gold as Phoebus.
But what of my estate now? Look at me.

'A Vase of Flowers'

You looked so tragic there
etched in black and grey
standing up despite it all
one broken stem
petal edges cutting
across the cross-hatch

the upturned faces
denied your true trajectory
for what is vertical seems alive
and you were already half gone
your colours still vivid
in that vase in Bologna in 1936

what a ragged clutch you were
blossoms caught
between the pinks
the yellows
and the black
but still standing up

from the castle

unsex me now
my hands are covered
with blood and sperm
here I wait
madam in the castle
hands trembling
bulletins assailing me
insects webbing my skin
tracings goadings
carrying me into
this farting marsh
the frit thicket
where branches kindle substances
of many and others
come before
come after
and there in the wall is the face of the one
and the faces of those who send their messages
and come directly to me
until the pricklings of my burnt skin
spell out the high numbers
while the soil-clogged
smoke-choked mouths
rut still in the fecund ooze

Grindelwald

a tiny calyx against his thumb
starry saxifrage
archangels
three kinds of sainfoin

barely a mountainside
but it looks like a castle
has exploded all over it

crouching amidst the rubble
he counts the campanulas
trumpet gentians
rock jasmine
moss campion
all those ferns
dryopteris and gymnocarpium

Jana leads the way
through the rocks and vetch

she knows just where to find
the things he has come to see

he watches
as her narrow back recedes
the bones beneath her skin
manoeuvring like creatures
under soft sand

**Topographical Guide to the
Nymphs of Great Britain and Ireland**

*the woods
    are not allowed*

*paths silent
    rivers curtailed*

twenty four classes
in this taxonomy
boxed up with a Bacchus in 1565
shipped
then released into faerie

```
in place of sadness
     of beauty
       of death
          of fields
            of rivers
               of flowers in pasture
               of flowers in water
                  of fish
                    birds
                      ice
                        clouds of every kind
                        six types of wind
                        blowing in like threats
```

Enumerate the seraphim
These nymphs and naiads
Orderly in their rank and line

    Erytheia   Ismene

        Philia   Alcyone

    Polyxo   Orea

        Rhodope   Oenone

  see her glistening tresses
     her white hands
       her upward glance
         her eyes like streams

  she will flit
    fly
      close her cool eyes
       live in oak and ivy
        dive in the earth
           air
             water
              unchained
               released
                free of repose
                  always lost

hear them dispute with gorse and gold
these decorous nymphs
what native charms they find
they will bury

their sweet murmurings
and lilting songs
will drown the clear voice
of the upland springs

remembering fern villages
  gatherings of nettles
    curling rivers
      paths that cannot be seen

scent of water earth
  of mere animals
    in the twitching green
      the sound filling up the air

in the strewn meadows
  dark river
    and flickering wood
      in the speaking hills

The invention of groves
Of glades and vistoes
A factory of pastoral
Fallen between trees

blinded by these new beauties
even our skies have flown

The Australian

at seventy mph
in the fizzing water
the bike skeets
across the gray-top

a droplet on a whale's back
streaking the surface
the Gillies Range
coming up on the right

*

it's warmer he said
behind the trucks
in the evil exhaust hinterland
where there is no air

and what air there is
is hot and you can't even see
the old grasses at the edge
of the road or beyond

*

when I met him years later
on the far side of the world
he told me he was at home
tucked in the slipstream

the Gillies Range coming up
the hot rain driving down
and over there in the mountains
he had said

there were thousands of plants
and different kinds of birds
which no one had ever seen
and no one ever would

Welcombe Mouth

I was on a number 38 bus
going down the South West Coast Path
towards Morwenstow
via Welcombe Mouth
with the stiles causing some difficulty
when I dinged the bell
and stopped off
at Ronald Duncan's little hut
by the nutty sea
where he wrote quite good poetry
and plays and stories
and even a film
and it occurred to me
while sitting inside
that its dimensions
were exactly the same
as those of the upstairs front
of a London omnibus
its big windows absorbing
not the lights, posters,
hidden rats and so forth
of Shaftesbury Avenue
but the black cliffs
white surf
and moiling grey waters
of a barbarous stretch
of Devon coastline
where not long ago
they hung lights on the cliffs
to lure ships to their doom
to lie there eviscerated
their treasures spilled
for all to purloin

and even now there are men
in the chip shops and pubs
who recall a wreck in the '80s
when they all went down
to Welcombe Mouth
and they all got something

a few miles on
the bus having negotiated
some tricky rocky passages
I discovered another hut
made by another poet
about 100 years earlier
the parson who smoked opium
and wore a pink hat
and kept a pig as a pet
I fell for his wooden shack
because it was so cosy and rude
like staring at the sea
from the portside cabin
and then I realised
its dimensions were the same
as the Vostok spaceship
which orbited the Earth
with Yuri Gagarin inside

out at sea a band was gathering
not of open-mouthed angels
but rain coming in low
bringing hailstones
some lightning
I could feel the deaths in the sea
the poets perched above
Gagarin even higher

and down there on the rocks
were all the riches laid out
for all to see and all to take
the leaky oil drums, split crates
jewelboxes, best brandy
everything and everyone
that someone might fall in love with
or want to take with them
before they go
and I thought about
getting down there quick
but knew the bus
would end up
just another wreck
caught on the rocks
and all its treasures flown

18/19

We were breathing in
the reddening folds
of that saloon
its intarsio and inlay work
visitors' book and trip advice
rose madder cushions
on the stiff legged sofa
the scent now gone of pot-pourri
ladling itself into the room
the furniture maneouvring around us
like oil tankers
a candelabra Cupid
above the fireplace
its carved marble surround
moving and fretting
on the vacant evenings
when between us we realised
we'd left something behind

Broadmoor Sirens

On Monday mornings the siren sounds
while the children are in handicrafts
sewing together soft pieces of felt,
the taste of the morning's milk
turning sour in their mouths
as the singsong siren calls out
from Crowthorne's covert.

It carries them away from the movements
of their hands and out into the tangled woods,
beyond the perimeter fence. Away
from their mothers and fathers
and into the domain of invisible birds
and rasping brambles. The places
where the madmen will be.

Why is it called the All Clear,
this siren which warns not of bombs
but of many and particular
kinds of madness? Incendiary minds
locked between carmine bricks
in Crowthorne's woods
in rapturous flower or silent dismay.

It is the electric herald of locked-up minds.
Of the men who will find us, it is said,
if we do not gather in the beeswax hall
when it grows dark and chill, where we are told
they have not found the man that is mad who escaped
that day when the siren sounded at the wrong time
and everything looked wrong including the teachers.

The siren speaks its warning. It tells
of those escaped and now on the loose,
traversing verdant Windsor Forest,
Pope's forest, where pheasants whir
past dryads and madmen, and sweet Lodona
is petrified in winter and in memory, lost in the hearts
of those who dwell now between the oaks.

The corridors and lawns grow grey.
Even the secretary's office is lost.
There is a madman on the loose.
He is out in the woods and in the fields,
quivering in makeshift shelters,
in drains and in culverts, trying back doors,
weeping in ditches, under corrugated iron.

The forest has gone mad. Its heady groves
are dead and cold. The stag's trampled tracks
are cracked cul de sacs. And Broadmoor's
siren no longer sounds. Yet still it sounds:
it cries for the nights of the mad
and for those who are out in the woods,
way beyond the perimeter fence.

Pick-a-dee

I don't know where I am
    parcels of trees
        grey earth
            the smell of a straight road

                    and the sheep lie down
                    in the sheep folds
                    they lie there neat and small
                    listen to the Mary bells
                    as the lambs lie down
                    in their rows

the age of bread and dripping
    thinnish jam
        yellow butter
            soft on willow pattern

                    Englefield Green
                    Stoke Poges or Datchet
                    Gertie wears velvet
                    compray your French

grey trees
    spindle trunks
        rubble soil
            a pate of brown sky

                    the bell rings out from the mairie
                    the car park is full of sheep
                    the folds are crammed
                    with crying white lambs
                    lying in rows privately

whiteness in the air
   and in the car parks
      low brick towns
         and wagon memories

a plum tree in Datchet
some iron in Slough
a picture in Englefield Green
the final air
of an actual day
out in Pick-a-dee

Lucie Rie Bakes a Cake

The children are playing in the mews
as Lucie talks of art
and mauls the mixing bowl
while the conversation turns.

The cake is warm; we like the cloy
and curranty squish, don't think
to notice what else it is
that Lucie has baked that day.

With crumbs round our mouths
we don't regard the cardboard box
on the passenger seat. Inside,
a new bowl, eggshell white.

old place

searching the grass for the children
   I knew I could not find
I saw a blur of golden hair
   heard running from behind

ripped apples in the orchard
   burst flowers on the path
and all around the treacling dusk
   coals smoking in the hearth

the corridor is darkish bright
   a golden landscape hanging
and in the parlour sitting still
   my godmother my darling

the queerest cat pads on the flags
   the roundel windows glowing
while outside all the little ones
   go blurring in their running

the boys

and so we went about
going place to place
finding stuff
smashing it up
getting bits and pieces
throwing it around
kicking things about
laughing at the old farts
shouting at the ugly cunts
never looking up
and so we went about   \ busy
like killers
smashing wrecked glasshouses
weak white skeletons
clinging on
in jagged orchards
sour rasp of apples
so bitter we retched
jumping down upon them
the splitting whiteness
the coming apart
right beneath our feet
all those fantastic deaths \ the
dawn bantams crowed
in the backs of the gardens
of the boys of the houses
where the cars have no wheels
and the men come and go
when the council van prowls
across bland afternoons
as we slip out of the road
to the flint-sharp alley
to recce the fields
go digging for spuds

paramilitary boys
with dirty old satchels
a little supplementary
some potatoes for dinner   \ porn
ripped-up in the rec
crumpled hair and skin
fragmentary cunt
fragmentary tit
unravelling before us
fleshly confetti
for greedy boys
messages from satyrs
wanking behind banks
of green shining laurel   \ the sky
a skein
flat thin on the fields
bleak stiles
indeterminate birds
retreat and repeat
fat black plastic sacks
strewn on the soil
cans crumpled in hedgerows
parades of blue bags
shaking in thornbushes
plastic cars reversing
into cuboid garages
fortresses of crap
dogs scratching at fences
barking at traffic
horses round corners
blowing and twitching
hooves on hard tarmac
O we were mad
like the animals   \ the violence
of tractors

bouncing down lanes
unsmiling drivers
gripping the plastic
men off to the fields
as they have done before
dead already
and all the time thinking
about how they will do it   \ down the lane
a murder
the smell of smoke
and the trees held back
gypsy on gypsy
no one knew what happened
gypsy business it was
they make their own laws
in the green man lane
on the far side of the village
well he must have stayed off
those gypsies have
no business
with no man of the forest   \ the elms
died the next year
the year that we lost it
trunks chewed up
by a maniac mouth
same smell in the fields
and the green man hulking

Landscape With Too Few Lovers (1986)

so nearly hand in hand
we walked down that flinty road
a watery delft sky
light bird traffic
brambles, plumping fruits
and all that

but then
we saw boucher maidens
hogarthian matrons and
crinkle crankle palmer trees
sprawling barrel-chested athletes
and sad young men walking in threes

and it seemed to me
that the white sky was lit up
'as if Arcturus himself had descended'

That was all some time ago (see title)
and here you stand before me again
the lumpen clodhopping ground
pulling me down like gravity

May Day in Dayton

Was it heat shimmer or petrol haze? I couldn't say. It was hot
that day in May, as we drove to your ex-workplace, the place
you inexplicably wanted to showcase, and I started to realize
that your eyes were half on the road ahead and your mind
only half on our conversation, the first we had had,
person to person, in a very long time. It became apparent
that the objects of your attention were in the air. You said
it was normal, there, to see helicopters in formation,
since the commercial airbase lay within the conurbation.
But still you weren't listening as I told my story, which
I had come all this way to say, and which you were treating
as something which could happen on just any other day.
Then I saw that you were glancing up through the windscreen
and that what you were noticing was the beginnings of a spin.
We heard the rotor speed slow and the helicopter going down
behind us, its tail beam scudding across the scrubby isthmus
low to the west, the blades still hissing. You stopped the car right there
on the freeway. Right there. We looked at the smoke, some way away,
and I thought of this day, and of how it would never ever go away.

the return of the yellow-robed monk

the king of spain has shot an elephant dead
and there he stands in his shorts and his balls

in the mist the black maria will roll over
allowing the criminals to abscond with dignity

not charles dickens's minor friend's descendant
the one I met over cheese and tomato

not the wood-turner and the wood-turner's mate
the backs of their necks reddened

not the record holder of world-record holdings
making a record, standing there with his pad

not the rectangular woman with the dangling bag
gathering up all that is crimson

oh, what a fanfare! — finally he arrives
the padre and his assailant . . . traversing . . .

/

it looked like a finely carved figure
but the ash was cruelly malformed

through the bars I travelled
wingèd beneath the shining bridge

midday under cassiopeia
they swaggered in ragged taffeta

zigzagging through the auditorium
the damp casket hidden inside

see the graph of outcomes
murmured by sentient forces of objects

as the visitors watch their season
go trundling down the plughole

/

so they made the switch
and it was tough, caked hide

running across the veldt
no sign of a joanna

the first leaf of the tract
it made a noise like lit fire

under the white pillbox tumbled
a few whole sprigs of her hair

unremitting slide
each tiny link catching the skin

/

grrrrrrrrrrrrrroooosssssss
our name for how we called it

inglorious technicolor
as reflected in snob glass

deep in the dell one wheel span
oh, the crown it will topple today

their heads among the pillows
another obscene prank

/

waving away the pickling jars
surely the evening cannot go awry

he readily agreed that it was All Too Much
for the *generalissimi*

but genealogy is just the start of it
try thinking about personality for once

/

that cave actually existed 35 metres
above where we are standing now

sometimes I get so emotional
this workroom it chokes me

/

at such a distance nothing is possible
therefore why not just hand it over

//

That French Novel

the one where the girl is corrupted
the one where the miners riot
the one where swordfighters prevail
the one where false optimism reigns

did you not know that it was real, that it would hurt,
that the world would keep on turning, that the story could
not go on

the one where a cad climbs socially
the one where an aesthete obsesses
the one where a giant does shits
the one where the novice has dreams

it was as we faltered that it suddenly became obvious to us
(for the politesse of your turnings met with so many
expectations)

the one where his wife is so restless
the one where a count is imprisoned
the one where the man eats some biscuits
the one where big nose wins out

it all seemed so real at the time and now we are disabused
your recommendations remain precious to me however

the one where a bellringer weeps
the one where the pilot crashes
the one where the clergy have passions
the one where an innocent's killed

nothing can be forgiven and there is nothing to forgive
a solemn equanimity must console us now

Gallery Girl *

Oh, Valerie, Valerie, gallery girl,
Your bosom is dainty, your skin is a pearl.
Up Cork Street then Bond Street you winsomely tread,
While I lie here, lovelorn, in Balham, in bed.

Oh, Valerie, Valerie, gallery girl,
You signed for my package, my passion unfurled;
As the catalogue's pages you gently depressed,
My earnest desire? To lift off your dress.

Oh, Valerie, Valerie, gallery girl,
From Cranborne to Rodean to Edinburgh Coll.,
Round boys and professors you've woven your spell,
Made history of art into exquisite hell.

Oh, Valerie, Valerie, gallery girl,
Here's oligarchs, magnates, playboys and earls.
'A bijou Brancusi, a Wallis on board —'
Is there nothing about you that I can afford?

Oh, Valerie, Valerie, gallery girl,
My body is keening, my head's in a whirl.
Such dolorous ennui, what delicious fatigue!
Yet it's plain as those price tags: you're out of my league.

* A Betjemanesquerie

Experimental Lady Poets of the 1920s

Experimental lady poets of the 1920s
I want to argue with you in slow bars
drink strong cocktails with no ice
disdaining the light outside
I want to see your eyes expand in rage
your long nose dilate and whiten
as we discuss with faux-solemnity
the avant garde and the rearguard
and what that has to do with Wisconsin

Experimental lady poets of the 1920s
as I admire your arms in the fraying light
the slighted angles of your dismayed coiffure
black fronds falling across your cheek
like those petals on a wet black bough
veiling eyes that hide dark similes
silken curlicues that smile but don't
while you tell of your high-minded meniality
the rouge on your cheeks a period detail

Experimental lady poets of the 1920s
yes I have an ulterior motive
since when we are done conversing
and the bar is shut and dry
we will spill outside and I shall find
a place to find your mouth your neck and
I will unfasten the girdle of your bemusement
agreeing all the while that the work will out
yes the work it will out

To William Shenstone

Twelve ash trees at a field's edge, ground sloping
north and upwards to a high dark covert;
mixed hedgerow — hawthorn, holly, three species
of finch — following the contour lines
ninety metres above a supposed sea.
Telegraph poles commute their language out
across counties; they say nothing of your
farm ornamental, your Virgilian groves.
Here lived your *Hamadryades*, nurses of
Ceres and *Bacchus*. Here played your *Naiades*,
delighting in waters, your *Napae* in
meadows and flowers. You knew them all by name.
Feel the caress of the breeze-nymphs, *Aureae*,
hear the anthems of the cloud-swathed *Nephele*.

How To Spend It

In here, you are lord and master, mistress and lady,
of all that you survey. Relax.

The decor is a little lurid — not exactly *World of Interiors*.
It's a bijou salon with a tinkling water feature.

Here is a place to hang your coat;
the security arrangements are state-of-the-art.

There's no need to meet the neighbours,
though you might hear them going about their business.

Here, you may pursue your philanthropic interests,
anonymous and unhindered, all day long.

Your unlimited wealth can be disposed of.
In here, you just give and give and give.

Examination of the Wengler Sisters in the Lecture Theatre of the Museum of Natural History, University of Leiden, March 15th 1762

From the topmost leaves of the limes in
the Houtstraat, bundles of green light tumble
down and into the embowered avenue
where claggy mud records last night's thunderstorm.

Propelled by an unlikely urban breeze,
a horde of young gentlemen flows beneath
the fluttering canopy towards the gateway
of the Museum of Natural History and thence

into a small parterre of box and narcissi
which some of the young gentlemen intend
to leap over, knowing the dread beadles are inside
busily preventing other young gentlemen

from scuffing the inlaid Brazilian teak and carob doors
which they like to kick open with their long-toed boots
as they progress through catalogued corridors filled with
splayed beasts, petrified ferns, stopped butterflies

and all the paraphernalia of this business of packaging up
the world, side by side with clocks, saints in agony
and the odd Madonna and Child or Rest on the
Flight to Egypt, while the air gilds itself with sunlight,

whorling and pitching above shining floors
which resound now with a dozen languages —
Swedish, Bavarian, Flemish, Catalan —
while the gentlemen brandish sheaves of papers

or sharpen their quills with little knives,
trying out jokes in Latin (dirty jokes,
to tell later with beer) until, after the final
dog-leg turn and spiral stair, suddenly

wigs are donned, expressions mended, mouths shut,
and the young gentlemen cram inside and arrange themselves
along the topmost rail of the lecture theatre,
craning down to see the grey heads and the bald heads

of professors and men of science, gowned and expectant,
like hunched herons waiting to fly, eager to hear
what Professor Jussieu (from Paris) has to say
about the singular physiology of the aberrations

Hilde and Louise Wengler, ditcher's daughters,
who hail from the little town of Heist-aan-Zee,
who have been conjoined since birth,
sharing a single urinary tract and,

they are informed, several vital organs
including heart and kidneys, although the truth
about their unhappy anatomy will only be
gleaned after their deaths which will, it is assumed,

be simultaneous, an anticipated occurrence
about which the physician expounds at length
before instructing his assistants to remove
the rough woollen blanket which covers

the modesty of the girls, who now raise
their eyes to the assembly and declare,
in their curious single voice: 'Our father
says we are all the children of God.'

Peter?

He stalks across the room
as if about to conduct,
wisps of white hair
dancing,
catching the eddies
like microlites.

Spry in his brown ones,
he appears to be
bouncing
bouncing
on the carpet –
the corduroy oom-pah!

Brown leather satchel,
slimline, shining . . .
shining like shoes.
Here he comes.
His ever-ready body declares:
'The world is my amuse bouche.'

Where are you going?
Where *are* you going?
If you are hatching
a plan, or a scheme,
I'd like to be in on it.
Peter?

Valete

People are outside
  but no fire alarms; it's only sunny.
      Tall buildings flicker.
          'I always feel most religious
          on a sunshiny day.' That's
          what Lord Byron said.

There are the lovers,
  lighting cigarettes.
      I remember when we
          blew smoke at each other
          like that, mingling
          our dirty souls.

Now we stare at the adverts,
  holding hands,
      transparently out of love.
          No bells sound from towers.
          Lord Byron is sunbathing.
          Birds fly individually about.

At Asheham

In the shrieking house
I thought about Monday
when this place would be done with
the reeking dump beyond the trees
moving closer by the hour
a ravenous midden
pounced upon by growling beasts
raked by exultant gulls

I walked up and over to view
the constant falling away
a sick note rising in my craw
and then I knew that what was
lobed in the windowframes
was not honey

Back Story

window or aisle: which will it be
take him out the back and shoot him

what do you want to achieve here
take him out the back and shoot him

nothing I can say about that
take him out the back and shoot him

I don't drink and I don't do drugs
take him out the back and shoot him

I can smell the smoke in your hair
take him out the back and shoot him

I recall dark trees and ploughed fields
take him out the back and shoot him

I can feel umbels of ivy
take him out the back and shoot him

ploughed fields and running after crows
take him out the back and shoot him

QUIET FOR THE WOUNDED

quiet for the wounded
quiet for the wounded
turn off those engines
so all the coppers shout
all down stamford street
all down the strand
it's quiet for the wounded

quiet for the wounded
children being scolded
buses stopping dead
coming on the boat train
shipping back to England
quiet for the wounded
back to waterloo

quiet for the wounded
rattling through the north downs
haslemere and guildford
green fields bowling by
bowling by the windows
all the blinded windows
quiet for the wounded

can you hear the field guns
all along the river
listen to them pounding
England's silent lanes
quiet in Westminster
quiet in Piccadilly
quiet for the wounded
we can never speak again

Maison Awkward

the loss of which
was not a blow to me
its fleeting nature being
part of its allure

or so I told myself
in the language of the
'How To Win In Love
(Again)' mag supp

those asteroids
so 1980s
your neo Georgian face
small and vivid in the room

later you would descend those steps
with such care
that I forgot I ever
knew you at all:

the cracked formulae moving
from room to room
sheet after sheet
of self-sacrifice

Endsleigh Pink

Eager for your news I read your letter,
a child in my arms — our child, you know it —
and all the chill of this desolate place,
these rooms, the doors, the looks of our people,
all of it vanishes, dissipates
with your sweet voice, your voice in my hands.
And I do so wish now that I could speak to you
as you used to do on our walks to me.

There was a tall Indian chestnut once
at the end of the high path named Georgy.
After rain you could sense the river there,
sliding uphill through the mossy trunks.
And hanging from branches all around,
pink bombarded rhododendron flowers.

Camden Morning

animals are expiring
all over the roads
splayed feathers recreating
Sydney Opera House

down on the high street
it smells like hangover
the heat an affront
to those without sleep

the fruit and veg men
are making their noises
maternally arranging
soft things in cradles

we drink coke with ice
and talk after a fashion
looking in people's eyes
to see if they're among us

there are fists up the walls
in the Halfway House
the hands of boxers
hovering like blessings

A Bowl of Fruit

taken from the clifftop
  the pittings looked
      insurmountable
          in spite of the slicking
          the barbs on the mend
          rattling away
          somewhere beneath us

a curve
  in the air
      leading deeper inside
         the light coming through
         greens
         and yellows
         laconic with the tide

loosening their ways
  the unseen numbers
      paralysed
         wholly planar
         courageously scrabbling
         around the very tops
         mouthing what was before

hovering airwards
  then out
      to the pale